How to PRAY *for the* GOVERNING AUTHORITIES

God's Rescue Plan for America

STEPHEN FRASER

How To Pray For the Governing Authorities
ISBN-13: 978-1-7350021-0-1

Copyright © 2009, 2020 Immerse Publications
First edition 2009. Second edition 2020.
Published by **Immerse Publications** - a division of Life of Faith Bible Church & Stephen Fraser Ministries
14200 Spegal Lane | Louisville, KY 40299 | lofbc.org | 888-542-2555

Printed in the United States of America. All rights reserved under International Copyright Law. Contents and/or cover may not be reproduced in whole or in part in any form without the express consent of the publisher.

Unless otherwise indicated, all Scripture quotations are taken from the ***New King James Version***®, Copyright© 1982 by Thomas Nelson, Inc. Used by permission. All rights reserved.

Scripture quotations marked (KJV) are taken from the ***King James Version*** of the Bible

Scripture quotations marked (AMP) are taken from the ***Amplified Bible,*** Copyright © 2015 by The Lockman Foundation. Used by permission. www.lockman.org

Scripture quotations marked (AMPC) are taken from the ***Amplified Bible,*** Copyright © 1954, 1958, 1962, 1964, 1965, 1987 by The Lockman Foundation. Used by permission. www.lockman.org

Scripture quotations marked (NLT) are taken from the ***Holy Bible, New Living Translation,*** copyright © 1996, 2004, 2007 by Tyndale House Foundation. Used by permission of Tyndale House Publishers, Inc., Carol Stream, Illinois 60188. All rights reserved.

Scripture quotations marked (ERV) are taken from the ***Easy-To-Read Version.*** Copyright © 2006 by Bible League International. Used by permission. All rights reserved.

Scripture quotations marked (NIV) are taken from the ***Holy Bible, New International Version***®, **NIV**®. Copyright© 1973, 1978, 1984, 2011 by Biblica, Inc.™ Used by permission of Zondervan. All rights reserved worldwide. zondervan.com

Scripture quotations marked (GNT) are from the ***Good News Translation*** (***Today's English Version,*** Second Edition) Copyright© 1992 American Bible Society. All rights reserved.

Scripture quotations marked (GW) are taken from **GOD'S WORD**®, © 1995 God's Word to the Nations. Used by permission of God's Word Mission Society.

Scripture quotations marked (CJB) are taken from the ***Complete Jewish Bible***® by David H. Stern. Copyright © 1998. All rights reserved. Used by permission of Messianic Jewish Publishers, 6120 Day Long Lane, Clarksville, MD 21029. www.messianicjewish.net.

Scripture quotations marked (CEB) are taken from the ***Common English Bible***®, Copyright © 2011. All rights reserved. Used by permission of Abingdon Press, Nashville, Tennessee.

CONTENTS

1. How to Survive the Storm 1
2. The Power of the Blessing 11
3. The Media Threat 19
4. What Do the Scriptures Say? 27
5. Releasing God's Judgment 35

References 49

About the Author 51

CHAPTER 1

HOW TO SURVIVE THE STORM

Rising out of the east and sweeping across the Atlantic Ocean like a mighty tempest, the influence of atheistic communism has made landfall in America. Its winds, waves, and heavy rains are already being felt throughout the nation, with the eye of the storm set upon the Capital and even the White House. In the twentieth century, this same deluge eroded freedom from some of the world's largest and most populated continents. Now, its storm surge threatens the freest nation in history. What can stem its tide and ultimately dissipate this tempest? The Bible makes the answer clear: It's the prayers of the righteous! James 5:16 declares that "the earnest (heartfelt, continued) prayer of a righteous man makes tremendous power available [dynamic in its working]" *(AMPC)*.

Humanism vs. Patriotism

Communism, socialism, and atheism are political names for their age-old spiritual counterpart, *humanism*—an ideology that stresses the potential power, values, and goodness of human beings, emphasizing "common human needs and seeking solely rational ways of solving human problems."[1] Humanism promises a one-world utopia if all nations would come together and unite under one banner or flag. This, of course, would require the elimination of individual sovereign nations. In this world view, to pledge allegiance to only one of the many nations or flags throughout the world is considered divisive and even fascist—the focus instead should be upon the worldwide human race, not the members of any one country.

Although this way of thinking has recently grown in popularity, it is not new. We see it at work even as far back as The Book of Beginnings, in Genesis chapter 11.

> Now the whole earth had one language and one speech. And they said, "Come, let us build ourselves a city, and a tower whose top is in the heavens; let us make a name for ourselves, lest we be scattered abroad over the face of the whole earth." But the Lord came down to see the city and the tower which the sons of men had built. And the Lord said, "Indeed the people are one and they

> all have one language, and this is what they begin to do; now nothing that they propose to do will be withheld from them. Come, let Us go down and there confuse their language, that they may not understand one another's speech." So the Lord scattered them abroad from there over the face of all the earth, and they ceased building the city. Therefore its name is called Babel, because there the Lord confused the language of all the earth; and from there the Lord scattered them abroad over the face of all the earth.
>
> —GENESIS 11:1, 4–9

Notice, it was the Lord who divided the world's population into individual nations, each with their own language and culture. Those who wanted to build a one-world society also wanted to redeem themselves by creating their own way of salvation, or way to heaven. Many people today continue to embrace these basic humanistic ideas. They look to their fellow man for peace and eternal security instead of looking to God. Attempting to save humanity, as well as the whales, the trees, and planet, these people adamantly oppose a strong devotion to God and country. They demonize patriotism, calling it racism, xenophobia, or extreme nationalism.

Later in Genesis, we see God saying to Abraham, "I will make you a great nation; I will bless you and make your name great; and you shall be a blessing" (12:2). Here we learn it was God's idea to make a nation out of the Jewish people. Then God said to Abraham, "As for Me, behold, My covenant is with you, and you shall be a father of many nations" (Gen. 17:4). Since the beginning, God has never sought to meld all the peoples of the world into one nation. He has always sought to make "many nations." Nowhere in Scripture does God say anything about the removal of nations, nor does He disapprove of the existence of different nations. On the contrary, He says, "God reigns over the nations . . ." (Ps. 47:8a).

> Since the beginning, God has never sought to meld all the peoples of the world into one nation. He has always sought to make "many nations."

Moreover, the Scriptures reveal that nations are recognized in heaven and will continue throughout eternity:

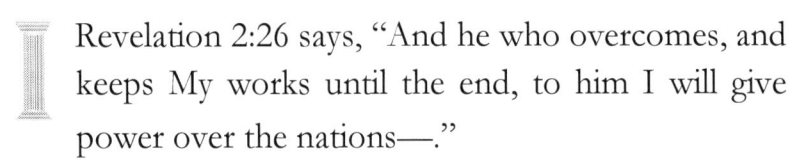

> Revelation 2:26 says, "And he who overcomes, and keeps My works until the end, to him I will give power over the nations—."

Revelation 7:9 says, "After these things I looked, and behold, a great multitude which no one could number, of all nations, tribes, peoples, and tongues, standing before the throne and before the Lamb, clothed with white robes, with palm branches in their hands."

Revelation 21:22-26 says, "But I saw no temple in it, for the Lord God Almighty and the Lamb are its temple. The city had no need of the sun or of the moon to shine in it, for the glory of God illuminated it. The Lamb is its light. And the nations of those who are saved shall walk in its light, and the kings of the earth bring their glory and honor into it. Its gates shall not be shut at all by day (there shall be no night there). And they shall bring the glory and the honor of the nations into it."

It would be wise for believers to search the Scriptures to know what the Bible has to say on this subject (and every subject) rather than to go along with any kind of political or cultural trend.

The Pledge of Allegiance

As humanism becomes more popular in America, the act of dishonoring our national anthem and flag will also increase in intensity. Most do not realize the significance of having our own flag; it is not only patriotic, but it is also scriptural and, therefore, of God. Consider Psalm 20:5b (*CEB*), which says, "We will fly our flags in the name of our God. Let the Lord fulfill all your requests!" This statement is similar to America's Pledge of Allegiance, which pays tribute to the flag and declares we are "one nation under God." "The Star-Spangled Banner" is a song about our country's fight for freedom. The lyrics remind us of how the flag served as a rallying point for those who fought against tyranny. In general, flags have long served as rallying points, and our nation's flag is still a rallying point for us today. We see this in Psalm 60:4; here are three different translations of this verse to help us fully understand its meaning:

> *Common English Bible*: "Give a flag to those who honor you, so they can rally around it, safe from attack."

> *Easy-to-Read Version*: "But you have provided a flag to show your faithful followers where to gather to escape the enemy's attack."

> *GOD'S WORD Translation*: "Yet, you have raised a flag for those who fear you so that they can rally to it when attacked by bows and arrows."

The American flag is meant to be a symbol of unity, not of racism and division. By it, we are to rally together.

The flag is also a symbol to our enemies, both spiritual and natural, that we are united together under God to defeat them. Therefore, it is ignorance to despise our flag in the name of wanting a united world. You cannot have a united world if you can't even unite with those of your own nation. The Bible teaches that "if a house is divided against itself, that house cannot stand" (Mk. 3:25). If a country is divided against itself, even due to its so-called "zeal for the world," that country will not stand. The key to saving the world is to first take a stand for your own nation.

Although God loves the whole world, He seeks to save it one nation at a time, starting with the nation of Israel. In Romans 1:16, the Apostle Paul wrote, "For I am not ashamed of the gospel of Christ, for it is the power of God to salvation for everyone who believes, *for the Jew first and also for the Greek*" (emphasis mine). Jesus said to His disciples, "But you shall receive power when the Holy Spirit has come upon you; and you shall be witnesses to Me in *Jerusalem, and in all Judea and Samaria, and to the end of the earth*" (Acts 1:8, emphasis mine). Reaching the world starts with reaching your neighbor, then your community, then your city, your region, and your nation. As a united nation, we can then reach other nations and ultimately the whole world. America has sent more missionaries around the world with the gospel than any other nation. We have been a beacon of light and hope. Our flag embodies this reality. To dishonor the flag is to deny our faith in the very God in whose name we fly our flag.

It is important to recognize that the spirit of humanism cloaks itself in false humility and racial justice. Instead of agreeing with people who embrace humanism or espouse humanistic ideals, we (regardless of race or gender) must rally together around our flag, declaring, "We are one nation under God with liberty and justice for all!" It is hypocritical to say you stand for racial justice if you despise and dishonor the very flag and pledge that symbolize "justice for all." To pledge allegiance to the flag of the United States of America, is to pledge allegiance to our fellow citizens—it is a statement of faith in God and a commitment to one another. It says to our fellow citizens, "You can count on me!" It also tells our enemies, both domestic and foreign, "Don't tread on me; I am united with my fellow countrymen against any attempt to undermine the faith and freedom we have in God." Remember, united we stand but divided we fall. So, with the clarity of Scripture, let us fearlessly and unashamedly pay our respects to the flag that unites us and pray for our nation.

Through prayer, we have access to the highest and most powerful government anywhere—we have access by faith into the very throne room of the King of all kings. It is Jesus Himself who said, "Therefore I say to you, whatever things you ask when you pray, believe that you receive them, and you will have them" (Mk. 11:24). Having been given such a promise, there can be no doubt about the power of prayer. Prayer is like having a security clearance into heaven's "war room"—a place full of the most sophisticated intelligence equipment and weaponry. This is not a place to come hoping and wishing you can make a difference. This is a place to come *in faith*, knowing you have what it takes to change anything.

> Prayer is like having a security clearance into heaven's "war room"—a place full of the most sophisticated intelligence equipment and weaponry.

This book is a spiritual "briefing" on how to rescue, restore, revive, and rally a nation back to the principles that made it great. This material has been declassified, so to speak, and made available to a generation of prayer warriors like you. By following its instructions, we will witness one of the most powerful displays of heaven on earth that has ever been!

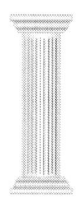

CHAPTER 2

THE POWER OF THE BLESSING

It's one thing to know that prayer contains the power to change circumstances, but it's another thing to know *what* to pray and *how* to pray. In First Timothy, the Apostle Paul reveals to us the best way to pray for our country—and that is by praying for its leaders.

> Therefore I exhort first of all that supplications, prayers, intercessions, and giving of thanks be made for all men, FOR KINGS AND ALL WHO ARE IN AUTHORITY, that we may lead a quiet and peaceable life in all godliness and reverence. For this is good and acceptable in the sight of God our Savior, Who desires all men to be saved and to come to the knowledge of the truth.
>
> —1 TIMOTHY 2:1-4 (emphasis mine)

Now that we know *who* to pray for, the big question is, *how* should we pray for them? I have found that many Christians pray for their government leaders by asking for God's blessing to be upon them. Their prayers sound something like this: "O God, thank you for our leaders. Bless them and their family. Help them to make wise decisions today. Give them guidance, strength, and favor." The Scriptures, however, do not teach that we should automatically pray for God to bless government officials. Yet, this is what so many praying believers feel obligated to do. This habit likely stems from the many Bible verses that teach us to honor our leaders; for example, First Peter 2:17 says, "Honor all people. Love the brotherhood. Fear God. Honor the king."

The phrase "to honor" means *to esteem and respect someone*.[2] God calls upon us to esteem and show respect for all governing authorities. However, being respectful and esteeming their office is not the same as blessing them. A *blessing* is more than just a religious way of saying something nice. The phrase "to bless" in the Old Testament means *to endue with power for success, prosperity, fruitfulness, richness, productiveness and longevity*.[3] The Blessing's major function seems to be to confer abundant and effective life upon something or someone. Proverbs 10:22 declares, "The blessing of the Lord makes one rich, and He adds no sorrow with it." It is the blessing of God that makes one successful at what he or she does in life.

In the Book of Numbers, the Bible gives an account of a king by the name of Balak, who sent messengers to a spiritus, or sorcerer, by the name of Balaam. Balak wanted Balaam to curse Israel because Balak feared that Israel would overpower him in battle. In Numbers 22:6, Balak says to Balaam, "Therefore please come at once, curse this people for me, for they are too mighty for me. Perhaps I shall be able to defeat them and drive them out of the land, for I know that he whom you bless is blessed, and he whom you curse is cursed." Here we see that the spiritual authority to bless was so real and effective, the King of Moab diligently sought to receive it from Balaam. Later in the story, God severely rebukes Balaam for attempting to use this spiritual authority against His people Israel.

The power to bless is so powerful, if we do not use it correctly, we might end up blessing (empowering to prosper with success) that which is contrary to God. We must understand and believe that what we bless is blessed, and what we curse is cursed. Having not understood its spiritual authority, the Church-at-large has foolishly blessed, and thus assisted, many demon-inspired plans of man. We must be watchful not to speak blessings over those who hold an agenda that is clearly against Christ and against the basic teachings of the Bible.

> We must be watchful not to speak blessings over those who hold an agenda that is clearly against Christ and against the basic teachings of the Bible.

How then are we to pray for our governing authorities? We are to pray for them with the intention of achieving the scriptural purpose for our praying. First Timothy doesn't just tell us *who* we are to pray for, but it also tells us *why* we are to pray for them: "that we may lead a quiet and peaceable life in all godliness and reverence" (2:2). Our praying, therefore, is not to be focused on a ruler for the sake of that ruler alone (for his personal well-being and success). Our praying for rulers is also for *our* success and well-being. God desires for us to live in a peaceful nation. Even in what many call "The Lord's Prayer," Jesus instructs us to pray for God's will to be done on earth just as it is in heaven (Matt. 6:10).

Many have believed that if something is God's will, it will automatically happen. However, if that were true, Jesus wouldn't be telling us to pray for it to be done. It is through our prayers that God works to bring His agenda to pass in the earth. It is not that God lacks the power, as in *strength* or *ability*, to bring His will to pass. But He may not have the power, as in *the authority*, to do so in a given situation. In the spiritual system He established, God needs a legal right to bring His plans to pass—He needs our prayers of faith.

Many people mistakenly believe that because God is sovereign, He can do whatever He wants to do whenever He wants to do it. If that were true, why did Jesus have to go to the cross, be tortured, and die a gruesome death in order to save us? Why didn't God just say, "I'm God; I want you forgiven; be forgiven" and then watch it come to pass? Apparently, His *will* (our redemption that He wanted to see happen) was not enough. In order for us to be justified and redeemed, Jesus had to pay the price for our sins with His own blood (Heb. 10:4), and we have to accept this sacrifice by faith and declare Jesus as Lord. Similarly, even though it is God's will to bless America, if we don't pray in faith, He won't be able to bring it to pass.

Be Watchful Who You Bless

And just because it may be God's will to bless our nation, that does not mean we should bless those who govern our nation. Why? Because there may be politicians whose agenda is contrary to our living a "quiet and peaceable life in all godliness and honesty" (1 Tim. 2:2). If their plans promote tyranny instead of freedom, fear instead of peace, wickedness instead of godliness, deception rather than honesty, we need to pray not for them to be blessed but for them to be stopped and their plans thwarted. We can also ask that they amend their ways and be reconciled to God.

However, praying that a leader would heed God and align his ways to God's ways can be in vain if that leader does not fear God nor have a heart to obey Him. God cannot lead and guide anyone against their will, regardless of how much we pray He would. Once again, this is not because He does not have the strength to do it, but because He does not have a legal right to do it apart from that person's own willingness to change. God is righteous, and He reigns according to what is morally right and just.

> God cannot lead and guide anyone against their will, regardless of how much we pray He would.

Throughout America's history, we have had leaders who, for the most part, have wanted to see America thrive. However, there are many in government today who do not seem to be seeking our well-being. Rather, they seek to exploit America's weaknesses for their own personal profit. Praying that God would guide such a leader is futile when it is clear the leader has no intention of following God's guidance.

There are some leaders today who are bent on overriding the Constitution and changing the culture of our country. When a leader seeks the advancement of ungodly practices, such as abortion and same-sex marriages, while enacting laws that forbid the right to speak out against such things, that leader needs to be respectfully rebuked and opposed. Even Michael the archangel of God respectfully rebuked Satan, who at that time (before Christ's victory at the cross) was the ruling spiritual authority over the world (*see* Luke 4:6). Before Jesus came and stripped Satan of his authority over mankind (*see* Colossians 2:15), Satan held a place of authority over this world that even the angel Michael respected. The Book of Jude gives us some insight into this dynamic: "Yet Michael the archangel, in contending with the devil, when he disputed about the body of Moses, *dared not bring against him a reviling accusation*, but said, 'The Lord rebuke you!'" (v. 9, emphasis mine). This clearly shows that we can be honorable and respectful towards authority while standing against them and even rebuking them.

We are not to pray for God to bless those who are seeking to destroy the very fabric of our nation's faith and freedom. It is time for the Church to pray in a way that will release angels like Michael to stand against the plans of those who have yielded themselves to Satan's influence. There are many such angels who are waiting our declarations of faith to do such things (*see* Hebrews 1:14). It is up to us to pray in faith and in line with Scripture, giving God access to accomplish His will in our lives, in our country, and in our world.

CHAPTER 3

THE MEDIA THREAT

When praying for those in authority over our nation, it is important to recognize another group of people who hold tremendous influence over the political process. Although they have never run for office or been elected through the voting process, they have taken a seat of authority over this nation—they are known as the mainstream media. While members of the media are not politicians, they wield the power of propaganda, which enables them to manipulate and control much of public opinion. These media outlets have held tremendous sway over elections. Through

> While members of the media are not politicians, they wield the power of propaganda, which enables them to manipulate and control much of public opinion.

intimidation, they have directed politicians and polices for years. Though they are not referred to as "governing authorities," they are, nonetheless, a type of governing authority in our country.

Until recently, the mainstream media has been a major voice in deciding who gets elected in our government and who does not. This should make us realize how important it is to pray for the members of the media as well as for our elected officials. Once again, I would not encourage people to pray prayers of blessing over anyone in the media who supports an anti-Christ, anti-American agenda. However, it would be scriptural to still pray for them—that their deceptive propaganda be exposed and that their power of influence be diminished.

The only problem here is that the Church cannot pray against that which it is entertained by! It is very unfortunate to see that much of the American Church today is mesmerized by the media in the same way that unbelievers are. Until we love righteousness and hate wickedness, our prayers against wickedness will not avail much. The truth is,

---
The truth is, what believers allow in their houses by means of the media (television, internet, etc.) they authorize to rule over them from the various houses of government.
---

what believers allow in their houses by means of the media (television, internet, etc.) they authorize to rule over them from the various houses of government. If we invite villains, deceivers, murderers, and thieves into our houses as "entertainment," how can we then stop them from ruling over us from the upper house (the Senate), the lower house (the House of Representatives), or the White House? Hypocritical prayers carry no weight in the eyes of God.

If we want our prayers to be heard, then we, God's people, who are called by His name, must humble ourselves and pray *and turn from our wicked ways* (2 Chr. 7:14), which may mean turning the channel or turning off our media device altogether. Praying without turning is not enough—we must turn from that which is contrary to godliness in our homes, *and then pray* for ungodly leaders to cease in the upper house, lower house, or the White House. This kind of *effective* praying will surely bring God's blessing and healing power upon our land!

Exposing Evil

One way God can heal our land is by removing from our government those who would seek to divide and conquer us through greed, perverseness, and humanistic philosophies. Not everyone has to be a Christian to qualify for a position in government, but everyone in government should have a fear of God or at least be sympathetic towards both the Church and the nation of Israel. We have seen leaders within our government deal gently with rogue nations who support terrorism, while dealing harshly with the nation of Israel (America's friend and faithful ally). Should we bless such leadership? Certainly not! There is a warning in the Scriptures against asking God to bless those who are haters of Israel: "Let all those who hate Zion be put to shame and turned back. *Neither* let those who pass by them *say, 'The blessing of the Lord be upon you; we bless you in the name of the Lord'"* (Ps. 129:5, 8 emphasis mine).

This passage clearly teaches us not to bless in the Name of the Lord those whose agenda is against Zion (Israel or the Church) and thus against Christ. So, when Jesus said to "bless those who curse you" (Matt. 5:44), He could not have been asking us to empower our enemies for success as they rise up against us. That would be self-destructive praying and inconsistent with other Scriptures. Rather, if we are going to bless an enemy that is opposing us, it is so they are empowered to

> If we are going to bless an enemy that is opposing us, it is so they are empowered to break free from Satan's deceptive hold on them.

break free from Satan's deceptive hold on them. This agrees with Second Timothy 2:25-26, which says, "In humility correcting those who are in opposition, if God perhaps will grant them repentance, so that they may know the truth, and that they may come to their senses and escape the snare of the devil, having been taken captive by him to do his will."

One of the ways members of the media may be helped to come to their senses and understand the truth, is by having their evil practices exposed and brought into the light for all to see. Sometimes the disgrace and downfall of a wicked person in the natural can be the best thing for them spiritually. For it would be better for them to hit rock bottom on the earth and to spend eternity reconciled to God, than to succeed in doing evil on earth only to spend eternity in the bottomless pit. Often, hell is referred to as "the bottomless pit" because all who go there never hit bottom and come to their senses. If they fall and hit bottom here on earth, they could actually turn from their ways and cry out for salvation as David did in the Psalms: "Before I was afflicted I went astray, but now I keep Your word" (119:67).

I am not instructing anyone to curse those who rule contrary to godliness—such an action would not be honoring our leaders. Ecclesiastes 10:20a says, "Do not curse the king, even in your thought." The word used in the original Hebrew for "curse" also means *to make light, to treat with contempt, to dishonor.*⁴ Let us look at some other translations of this same verse to get a better understanding of the meaning of this word "curse."

- "Do not revile the king even in your thoughts" (*NIV*).

- "Don't criticize the king, even silently" (*GNT*).

- "Never make light of the king, even in your thoughts" (*NLT*).

Remember what we learned about the respect even the angels show: "Michael the archangel, in contending with the devil, when he disputed about the body of Moses, *dared not bring against him a reviling accusation, but said, 'The Lord rebuke you'*" (Jude 9, emphasis mine). So, we are not to revile or criticize and thus curse the king (the President or anyone in a position of authority). Acts 23:5 tells us, "You shall not speak *evil* of a ruler of your people" (emphasis mine). However, this does not mean we cannot disapprove of their words or condemn their actions. The word used in Jude for "rebuke" also means: *to express strong disapproval of someone, to denounce* ⁵*(condemn, censure).*

It is true that opposing someone by expressing strong disapproval of them can appear to be criticizing or reviling them, but as we saw with the archangel Michael, *rebuking* is one thing and *reviling* is something else. One is honorably confronting and dealing with *a problem*, while the other is insulting and mistreating *the person*. Objecting to someone's words or actions does not have to be obnoxious and hateful. Rebuke should not be considered "hate speech" when it comes from a heart of concern for others.

I believe if we walk in a critical spirit before others, it will prevent us from praying in the right spirit before the Lord. Let us lay hold of this balance and diligently present ourselves before the Lord in prayer concerning those who govern our nation. Let us believe God that anyone whose policies undermine our leading a quiet and peaceable life in all godliness and honesty will be stopped and replaced. It is time to ask God to bless America by delivering us from leaders who are set against the blessing of God upon our country.

> I believe if we walk in a critical spirit before others, it will prevent us from praying in the right spirit before the Lord.

In praying for the media, we need to ask God to raise up opposition so that ungodly messages and messengers no longer lead the people of our nation astray. We need to ask that any media outlet that embraces an ungodly agenda be replaced by those who fear God. And we need to pray for revival in the Church, so believers will no longer support the media by being entertained like the rest of the world. May the Lord hear our prayers and grant our nation mercy for the sake of the righteous who are in it.

I encourage you to let your voice be heard on High concerning these things, for every prayer of faith counts in heaven. I believe that if we are led by the Holy Spirit in this matter, we will help to advance those in government who should be advanced and stop the progress of those who should be prevented from leading.

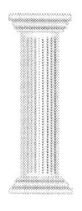

CHAPTER 4

WHAT DO THE SCRIPTURES SAY?

In the Old Testament, before taking the throne as King of Israel, David was pursued by his political predecessor King Saul. Saul sought to destroy David's life because he knew the Lord had anointed David to be the next king in his place. Although Saul continually sought to harm David, David never raised his hand against Saul, stating, "The Lord forbid that I should do this thing to my master, the Lord's anointed, to stretch out my hand against him, seeing he is the anointed of the Lord" (1 Sam. 24:6). Later in the same chapter, David again says, ". . I will not stretch out my hand against my lord, for he is the Lord's anointed" (24:10b). David comments on this subject several times: ". . . for who can stretch out his hand against the Lord's anointed, and be guiltless?" (1 Sam. 26:9b). And, "The Lord forbid that I should stretch out my hand against the Lord's anointed . . ." (1 Sam. 26:11a). David paid the highest respect to the King and to all his leaders.

David showed this respect even when Saul was trying to kill him. However, notice some of the things David said by the Holy Spirit when he prayed for the King and those in authority:

> "I will cry out to God Most High, to God who performs all things for me. He shall send from heaven and save me; He *reproaches* [rebukes, defies, upbraids][6] the one [the king] who would swallow me up" (A prayer of David when he fled from Saul into the cave. Ps. 57:2-3, emphasis mine).

> "My God of mercy shall come to meet me; God shall let me see my desire on my enemies. Do not slay them, lest my people forget; *scatter them by your power, and bring them down*, O Lord our shield. For the sin of their mouth and the words of their lips, *let them even be taken in their pride*, and for the cursing and lying which they speak. *Consume them in wrath, consume them, that they may not be*; and let them know that God rules in Jacob to the ends of the earth (A prayer of David when Saul sent men, and they watched the house in order to kill him. Ps. 59:10-13, emphasis mine).

"Let his days be few; and let another take his office" (Ps. 109:8).

Here we see David praying for God to intervene on his behalf, to preserve his life and remove Saul from power. Again, this kind of praying does not in itself imply ill will, but this is consistent with the purest goodwill, the kindest feelings, the strictest integrity, the sternest patriotism, and the highest form of piety. These are faith-filled, Holy-Spirit inspired words recorded in Scripture for our learning. They are given that we may use them in prayer when deemed appropriate by the Holy Spirit. There is nothing dishonorable about praying this way concerning those abusing their authority—if there were, David would not have been inspired by the Holy Spirit to pray this way. Neither would this be in the Bible as an example for us to learn from.

Unlike David, there are many people today who loudly express contempt for any leader who rules contrary to what they want. They revile, criticize, slander, and viciously mock them—and seem to be willing to do anything to destroy them. Their shouts to resist authority are more than a rebuke of authority; it is rebellion. Fortunately, we have promises that we can mix with our faith to deal with such anarchy in our nation.

The Bible states, "Therefore whoever resists the authority resists the ordinance of God, and those who resist will bring judgment on themselves" (Rom. 13:2). When people stray far away from what is right, sometimes the best thing that can happen to them is judgment. Judgment is not the hand of God coming down upon a person in punishment. Actually, it is the result of people getting out from under His hand—for God's hand is full of love and mercy. Persisting in rebellion will take you out from under His hand of protection. Judgment can be simply defined as reaping the consequences of your sin. Mercy is the opposite; mercy is being kept from those consequences.

When we see government leaders, media outlets, or activists leading a rebellion against leaders of our country, it is important to call them out in prayer. Many times, I will release my faith in the Scriptures by saying the name or names of those who are leading the rebellion, and I pray something such as this: "Father, you said that 'those who resist authority will bring judgment on themselves' (Rom. 13:2), so I thank You that [So-and-so] reaps what they sow. I thank You that 'those who seek to dig a pit, will themselves fall into it; and those who roll a stone will have it rolled back on them' (Prov. 26:27). I pray that the very things they have sought to do are now happing to them." This prayer might sound harsh, but it is scriptural (both Old and New Testaments).

There is a time for mercy and a time for judgment—knowing *what* is right and *when* it is right is getting easier to discern. Many people who sought to portray themselves as patriotic are now openly showing a radical resistance to the Constitution and traditional values. And those who have called themselves "liberal" are clearly showing themselves to be greedy for all the money and power they can get from their constituencies. The Bible predicted this very thing, prophesying a time when "the vile person shall be no more called liberal . . . for the vile person will speak villainy, and his heart will work iniquity, to practice hypocrisy, and to utter error against the Lord . . ." (Isa. 32:5-6, *KJV*).

If the Bible says it like it is, then so should we. This is not the time to hide our heads in the sand and just pray a general prayer of blessing over our nation. Instead, we must see what God sees and say what He says when we pray. It is through our praying that injustice and corruption can be judged and removed from our land.

The Ousting Outcry of Faith

Most believers know about the judgment that came upon Sodom and Gomorrah. However, many people do not stop to consider why they were judged. It was not merely because they were wicked and perverse; it is evident from their behavior that they had been that way for a long time. What, then, brought them to their end? What caused judgment to finally come upon them? For the answer, let's look at the Lord's words to Abraham:

> And the Lord said, "Because the outcry against Sodom and Gomorrah is great, and because their sin is very grave, I will go down now and see whether they have done altogether according to the outcry against it that has come to Me; and if not, I will know."
>
> —GENESIS 18:20-21

Notice, the word "outcry" is mentioned twice in this brief passage. This outcry must have come from those who had God's ear in prayer. Abraham also had God's ear, and when he made intercession on behalf of the people of those cities, the righteous there were spared (even though it was only Lot and his two daughters).

We see the same thing happen concerning Egypt in the days of Moses. Egypt's government was exceedingly oppressive, yet nothing was done about it until an outcry from God's people reached His ear.

> Then the children of Israel groaned because of the bondage, and they cried out; and their cry came up to God because of the bondage. So God heard their groaning, and God remembered His covenant with Abraham, with Isaac, and with Jacob. And God looked upon the children of Israel, and God acknowledged them.
> —EXODUS 2:23-25

Although the Israelites must have been crying out to God for a very long time, what finally caused their cry to bring about divine intervention? It was their faith in His covenant promises. This is a major component in receiving answers to prayer—for it is in reminding God of what He promised us that we have the legal ground of faith to expect God to answer His promises. This is why the Lord said, "Put Me in remembrance; let us contend together; state your case, that you may be acquitted" (Isa. 43:26).

> We have the legal ground of faith to expect God to answer His promises.

Although God earnestly desires to deliver us immediately, He is restrained by His own laws. As we learned previously, God is just, therefore, He has to do everything legally. Our faith in His covenant is what gives Him the legal right to do what He Himself has desired to do all along. By knowing these truths, we will not have to wait until oppression escalates to the degree that it did in the governments of Sodom, Gomorrah, and Egypt. We can experience God's deliverance in the here and now.

CHAPTER 5

RELEASING GOD'S JUDGMENT

If you still feel uncomfortable about crying out to God for justice to be served, remember, this sort of cry is happening even in heaven. Revelation 6:10-11 says, "And they cried with a loud voice, saying, 'How long, O Lord, holy and true, until You judge and avenge our blood on those who dwell on the earth?' Then a white robe was given to each of them; and it was said to them that they should rest a little while longer, until both the number of their fellow servants and their brethren, who would be killed as they were, was completed." The Book of Revelation even tells of a time (possibly soon), when witnesses of Christ will release judgment upon the earth in the form of plagues (*see* Revelation 11:3-6). The Church of Jesus Christ must be bold in these last days. The world is growing more and more corrupt, and if we just pray little sweetie-pie prayers for God to bless everybody, we will be run over by the wicked.

One of the reasons why the believers in the Book of Acts were so successful is because they were feared. On his first missionary journey, the Apostle Paul pronounced temporary blindness on a false prophet who was deceiving the proconsul (a governor with much authority). Later, Paul turned an immoral man who was in the Church at Corinth over to Satan for the destruction of his flesh. Also, the Apostle Peter pronounced judgment on a couple in the church for lying to the Holy Spirit—and they immediately fell dead in front of everyone. And when a certain new convert wanted to make merchandise of the Anointing, Peter pronounced judgment over him saying, "Your money perish with you" (Acts 8:20). The man responded, "Pray to the Lord for me, that none of the things which you have spoken may come upon me" (Acts 8:24b).

Many teach that judgment went out with Old Testament and is not a part of the New Testament Church. However, such teaching is false. The New Testament even goes as far to say, "For the time has come for judgement to begin at the house of God; and if it begins with us first, what will be the end of those who do not obey the gospel of God" (1 Pet. 4:17).

Check Yourself

It is important, of course, to judge *ourselves* before talking to God in prayer about *others*. We must first have clean hands before we can help clean our government. Trying to remove the speck from another person's eye, while having a glaring plank in our own, is hypocrisy—such prayers will not be effective (*see* Matthew 7; Luke 6). Such prayers may actually call for an audit of our own life, rather than bringing about change in others. The Bible states the order of things, saying, "being ready to punish all disobedience *when your obedience is fulfilled*" (2 Cor. 10:6, emphasis mine).

For our prayers to be effective, we need to first live the way we want our leaders to lead (in all godliness). If we have an "idol" propped up in the media room of our house, then we can't expect to have something other than wicked idol worshipers to rule over us—it is just a matter of reaping what we have sown (*see* Galatians 6:8). Furthermore, when we bring a case for judgment before the Lord, it is important to be accurate in our analysis of the one we are crying out to God about. For as the Lord said to Abraham, "I will go down now and see whether they have done altogether according to the outcry against it that has come to Me; and if not, I will know" (Gen. 18:21). If our crying out about others is just the result of our being personally offended, prideful, or whiny, we may bring judgment on ourselves. That is why James wrote, "Do not grumble against one another, brethren, lest you be condemned. Behold, the Judge is standing at the door" (Jas. 5:9, emphasis mine).

Keeping your heart right before God is key to praying safely and successfully, especially when bringing judgment against others. To do this, always be sure to check your "love gauge." Ask yourself the questions, *Do I love this person? Do I care about them?* Regardless of whether you are seeking mercy or judgment, make sure you are walking in love towards them first—for faith works by love (Gal. 5:6). It is possible to become so disgusted with people's evil actions, that you just want to see their downfall. When approaching God about having someone's wicked deeds backfire on them, you must make sure you are acting out of love and care for them—in wrath, remember mercy (*see* Habakkuk 3:2b). Let me restate: When seeking the diminishing or removal of a government official, it must not be from a heart of bitterness or unforgiveness; you must be motivated from love and hope, prayerful that their downfall will lead to their answering God's call to repent. We must always have a genuine concern for the souls of all people.

Caring about the eternal state of a wicked person is made easier when we remember that deceptive people are themselves deceived. Our Lord prayed from the cross, "Father, forgive them; for they know not what they do" (Lk. 23:34 *KJV*). We need to consider the spirit or spirits that are deceiving and ruling over ungodly rulers. Either the Holy Spirit is inspiring a person's actions or an evil spirit is. How can you know the difference? Anyone following an agenda against the Church, against Scripture, or against life is *against Christ*—which First

John 4:3 refers to as "the spirit of antichrist." Nobody becomes anti-Christ on their own without the help of evil spirits. Thank God, we have been given authority over such spirits in the Name of Jesus.

After His resurrection, Jesus commissioned those who believe in Him to cast out demons in His name. Therefore, your prayer time might not only involve a conversation between you and God. Many times while in God's presence, you will need to speak to the evil spirits or demons who are at work in those you are praying for. Although you may not be able to cast the devil out without that person's approval and cooperation, you can place a temporary restraining order, so to speak, on the evil spirits. Simply call the evil spirit (or spirits) out and command them to cease and desist in their maneuvers and operations in Jesus' Name.[7] Unless those who are under the influence of the devil repent or are removed from their place of authority and influence, you may need to renew your "restraining orders" against the devil on a regular basis.

It's important to remember that "our struggle is not against flesh and blood [contending only with physical opponents], but against the rulers, against the powers, against the world forces of this [present] darkness, against the spiritual forces of wickedness in the heavenly (supernatural) places" (Eph. 6:12 *AMP)*. In the Old Testament, the prophet Daniel received revelation concerning these spiritual forces—revelation that can help us as we pray.

While Daniel was praying for the Jewish people to be liberated from their oppressors, an angel appeared to him with a message.

> Then he [the angel] said, "Do you know why I have come to you? And now I must return to fight with the prince of Persia; and when I have gone forth, indeed the prince of Greece will come. But I will tell you what is noted in the Scripture of Truth. No one upholds me against these, except Michael your prince."
>
> —DANIEL 10:20-21

These angels were not fighting with human princes, or human rulers, of Persia and Greece. They were fighting evil spirits (principalities) who ruled over the human princes of Persia and Greece. Michael the archangel was one of the angels mentioned in this fight. In Daniel 12:1 he is called "the great prince who stands watch over the sons of your people [the Jewish people]". It is important to note that Michael doesn't come to a battle without his troops (other angels). Revelation 12:7 says, "Michael and his angels fought with the dragon [Satan] . . . ." (emphasis mine).

Israel's angel, Michael—*and* the angels under Michael's authority—were dispatched to assist the angel(s) fighting the evil spirits who were ruling over the countries of Persia and Greece. This warring in the heavenly places transpired *first*—before any change could take place among the people of those nations. And these spiritual battles and earthly changes were brought about through Daniel's continued, heartfelt prayers. Through his praying, Daniel waged a spiritual war that changed nations and ultimately liberated the Jewish people from their exile in Babylon. (The first chapter of Ezra mentions this liberation, recording the decree by Cyrus, King of Persia, to let the Jews return to their homeland.)

Daniel offers us an example to follow. Instead of addressing the human problems in government with mere human methods, we need to go to the root of our political problems. Second Corinthians 10:4 reminds us that "the weapons of our warfare are not physical [weapons of flesh and blood], but they are mighty before God for the overthrow and destruction of strongholds." Ephesians 6:12 tells us to come against the "principalities, against powers, against the rulers of the darkness of this age, against the spiritual hosts of wickedness in the heavenly places." According to Ephesians 3:10, the Church (the Body of Christ, or Christian believers) comes against these evil spirits in the heavenly places by making God's Word known to them: "To the intent that now the manifold wisdom of God [God's Word] might be made known by the church to the principalities and powers in the heavenly places"

Perhaps Jesus demonstrated the greatest example of this kind of spiritual warfare. After being led by the Spirit into the wilderness to be tempted by Satan, Jesus fought each attack by saying, "It is written" and then quoting Scripture. In His final counterattack, Jesus said to Satan, "Away with you, Satan! For it is written, 'You shall worship the Lord your God, and Him only you shall serve'" (Matt. 4:10). By calling the devil out, and speaking forth our faith in God's Word, we can stop Satan's maneuvers and seek to prohibit his tempting of government officials.

Many people mistakenly have the idea that because God is sovereign, He will stop whatever He wants stopped and make happen whatever He wants to happen. What they fail to realize is that God in His sovereignty gave mankind the authority, or dominion, over the works of His hands. In fact, God would be unjust to "do whatever He wanted" with that which He has given to us. The Bible says, "The heaven, even the heavens, are the Lord's; but the earth He has given to the children of men" (Ps. 115:16).

In the Garden of Eden, God placed the responsibility for what happens on the earth into the hands of man. However, the first man, Adam, sold out to Satan and surrendered authority over the earth to him. This made Satan the ruler of this world. Thankfully, in God's mercy, Jesus came to earth; He defeated death, hell, and the grave by stripping Satan of his authority over us. Now He declares, "I will give you the keys of the Kingdom of Heaven. Whatever you prohibit on earth will be prohibited in heaven, and whatever you permit on earth will be permitted in heaven" (Matt. 16:19 *CJB*).

If we do not use these keys of authority to prohibit evil spirits, then stealing, killing, and destroying will have free reign over us. This is how wicked regimes have risen to power throughout history, some having mercilessly destroyed millions of people. Dictators like Vladimir Lenin, Joseph Stalin, Mao Zedong, and Adolf Hitler (to name just a few) were completely given over to Satanic inspiration. History would be vastly different if people knew their God-given authority and took action in the spirit against such demonically motivated individuals.

What about us today? Will we sit back and allow politicians who have a track record of lying, stealing, and otherwise violating the Christian faith to continue to fester in our government? Through our understanding of how to pray for the governing authorities, we can make a crucial difference in the way things develop in America and around the world. Although the darkness is getting thicker, there is still time to turn the tide for our country's future.

> Although the darkness is getting thicker, there is still time to turn the tide for our country's future.

The Lord has promised in Ezekiel 20:38 "I will purge the rebels from among you, and those who transgress against Me; *I will bring them out of the country* where they dwell, but they shall not enter the land of Israel [or America]. Then you will know that I am the Lord" (emphasis mine). I encourage you to boldly and consistently pray for our leaders, that we may see the goodness of the Lord in the land of the living!

REFERENCES

1. "Humanism." *Oxford University Press.* 2020. https://www.lexico.com/en/definition/humanism (7 July 2020).

2. American Heritage® Dictionary of the English Language, Fifth Edition. Copyright © 2016 by Houghton Mifflin Harcourt Publishing Company. Published by Houghton Mifflin Harcourt Publishing Company. All rights reserved.

3. Strong, James. The New Strong's Exhaustive Concordance of the Bible. Nashville, TN: Thomas Nelson, 1984, s.v. "to bless"

4. W.E. Vine, Merrill, Unger, and William White Jr., An Expository Dictionary of Biblical Words (Nashville, TN: Thomas Nelson, 1984), s.v. "to curse", pg 53

5. Strong, James. The New Strong's Exhaustive Concordance of the Bible. Nashville, TN: Thomas Nelson, 1984, s.v. "rebuke"

6. Strong, James. The New Strong's Exhaustive Concordance of the Bible. Nashville, TN: Thomas Nelson, 1984, s.v. "reproach"

7. Hagin, Kenneth E., *How You Can Be Led by the Spirit of God, Legacy Edition* (Tulsa, OK: Kenneth Hagin Ministries, 2006) p. 73.

ABOUT THE AUTHOR

Living by faith in the dynamic grace of God has enabled Stephen Fraser to witness the salvation, healing, and deliverance of many people. He is currently the senior pastor of Life of Faith Bible Church in Louisville, Kentucky; a church he founded in 1994. As a television host and evangelist, he ministers daily through the "Living the Life" television broadcast. He is also the author of several books that bring fresh revelation to controversial subjects. Both he and his wife, Jeanne, minister with a powerful, prophetic voice while demonstrating the miraculous power of the Gospel.

Stephen's balanced teaching and unwavering faith cuts to the heart. His ministering is bold and convicting, yet refreshing and humorous as it ignites faith in all who hear him.

Request a
FREE CATALOG
for more books and materials by Stephen Fraser.

Call 1-888-542-2555
www.lofbc.org